Going Forth

St. Alphonsus de Liguori
and the Spirituality of Mission

Dennis J. Billy, C.Ss.R.

En Route Books and Media, LLC
Saint Louis, MO

⊛ENROUTE
Make the time

En Route Books and Media, LLC
5705 Rhodes Avenue
St. Louis, MO 63109

Contact us at
contactus@enroutebooksandmedia.com

Cover Credit: Sebastian Mahfood

Copyright 2026 Dennis J. Billy, C.Ss.R.

ISBN-13: 979-8-88870-496-7
Library of Congress Control Number: 2026932696

All rights reserved. No part of this book may be reproduced, stored in a retrieval system, or transmitted in any form, or by any means, electronic, mechanical, photocopying, or otherwise, without the prior written permission of the author.

For the
Redemptorist Partners in Mission

The most abandoned, to whom in particular the congregation is sent, are those for whom the Church has not yet been able to provide sufficient means of salvation, those who have never heard the Church's message, or at least do not receive it as the "Good News," and finally those who suffer harm because of division in the Church.

C.Ss.R. Constitution, no. 3

Table of Contents

Introduction 1

Chapter One: The Origins of Mission 5

Chapter Two: Mission in St. Alphonsus 27

Chapter Three: Preaching the Gospel 49

Chapter Four: Plentiful Redemption 67

Chapter Five: Poor and Most Abandoned 89

Conclusion 107

Introduction

In two of my previous works, *Holy Exercises* and *Paradise for God*, I treated respectively St. Alphonsus's "Spirituality of Practice" and the "Spirituality of Heart."[1] In this present work, *Going Forth*, I will examine his understanding of the "Spirituality of Mission" and thus bring to conclusion my trilogy on Alphonsian spirituality.

As you may recall, these three works were inspired by a veritable turning point in Alphonsus's life, when after much discernment and soul-searching, he knelt before an altar of Our Lady of Mercy in the church of Our Lady of Ransom in Naples, drew his nobleman's sword and laid it at her feet, promising her that, from then on, he would dedicate himself to the service of the Church as a Catholic priest. It was also inspired by a verse from *The Letter to the Hebrews*: "Indeed, the word of God is living and active,

---

[1] See Dennis J. Billy, *Holy Exercises: St. Alphonsus de Liguori and the Spirituality of Practice* (St. Louis, MO: En Route Books & Media, 2024) and Idem. *Paradise for God: St. Alphonsus de Liguori and the Spirituality of Heart* (St. Louis, MO: En Route Books & Media, 2025).

sharper than any two-edged sword, piercing until it divides soul from spirit, joints from marrow; it is able to judge the thoughts and intentions of the heart" (Heb 4:12).[2] Alphonsian spirituality, I claim, is itself like a two-edged sword, with one edge representing a "Spirituality of Practice," the other, a "Spirituality of Heart," and both edges coming together in a "Spirituality of Mission." Alphonsus's life as a priest was all about mission to the poor and most abandoned. The same holds true for the Redemptorists, the religious order he founded.

It would be a mistake to think that Alphonsus's spirituality can simply be taken out of its eighteenth southern Italian environment and applied to our situation today lock, stock, and barrel. As man of his times, Alphonsus was deeply embedded in the culture of his day, with all the strengths and weaknesses, accomplishments and failures that came with it. It would be equally wrong, however, to think that he has nothing to say to today's world. Consisting of five

---

[2] Unless otherwise stated, all Scripture quotations come from *Holy Bible: New Revised Standard Version with Apocrypha* (New York: Oxford University Press, 1989).

chapters, this book intends to examine the Redemptorist mission in the context of its stated purpose, "to preach plentiful redemption to the poor and most abandoned." Chapter one, "The Origins of Mission," examines the theological and anthropological roots of Christian missionary efforts in general. Chapter two "Mission in St. Alphonsus," focuses on Alphonsus's understanding of mission. Chapter three, "Preaching the Gospel," looks at Alphonsus's approach to preaching and its relevance for today. Chapter four, "Plentiful Redemption" considers the various levels of Christ's redemptive grace, its meaning, and its far-reaching consequences. Chapter five, "Poor and Most Abandoned" considers Alphonsus's understanding of this phrase and its relevance for today. My goal in this book is to interpret Alphonsus's understanding mission in a language that speaks to us today, while at the same time remaining faithful to his deepest insights about the spiritual life. I invite you, the reader, to accompany me on this journey of discovery, as we delve into Alphonsus's "Spirituality of Mission" and find its purpose and meaning for his followers today

Chapter One

The Origins of Mission

The Christian mission has its roots in the Triune mystery of the Godhead. Christians believe that "God is love" (1 Jn 4:8). His very nature, Existence Itself, embodies the innermost dynamics of love and are manifest in the threefold relationship of Father, Son, and Spirit: Three Divine Persons, sharing the same substance, yet existing in different relationships to one another. From all eternity, the Father generates the Son who, in turn, empties himself in obedience to the Father's will, and the Holy Spirit, who proceeds from the intimate and eternal bond of love between Father and Son. Christian missionary activity flows from the very nature of God himself and the threefold divine actions (or missions) typically associated with him: Creation, Redemption, and Sanctification. Although God always acts as one, Creation is typically associated with the Father; Redemption, with the Son; and Sanctification, with the Holy Spirit. These actions are fundamentally both free and good. In this chapter, we will see how Christian missionary activity flows from the nature and actions of the Triune God and relevance for us by virtue of the fact that we are created in God's image and likeness (Gn 1:26).

The Missions of the Triune God

As stated above, there are Three Persons in One God who share one divine nature yet are distinct from each other by virtue of their relationships. They exist beyond time and space, for he created them and sustains them from one moment to the next. They are within him rather than outside him and depend on him in creaturely fashion. The actions of God—Creation, Redemption, and Sanctification—are actions of his Love occurring in time and space and existing at the very core of his being. Because God is, at one and the same time, both One and Three, his actions are similarly One in Three. That is to say that these actions are simultaneously actions of the One God, yet typically associated with one of the Persons: Creation with the Father; Redemption, with the Son; and Sanctification, with the Holy Spirit. The act of Creation aligns with the Father because it resembles his eternal generative power; Redemption with the Son because it flows from his eternal kenotic self-emptying; Sanctification with the Holy Spirit because he embodies the infinite holiness that proceeds from the mutual love between the Father and his Son.

Because God is love, he wanted some part of his Creation to love him in return. Love, by its very nature, is self-diffusive and freely wishes to share itself with others. God created us in his image and likeness because he wanted us to be able to enter into an intimate relationship with him, that is, wishing to live in our hearts, so that we might live in his. He wants us to share in his divinity while still allowing us to remain a part of his Creation. What is more, because we are created in his image and likeness, he empowers us to spread his Love through similar (albeit derivative) missions of creation, redemption, and sanctification. Such is our purpose on earth: to share in God's creative, redemptive, and sanctifying activity. Be that as it may, the question arises: How is this so?

When asked what the greatest commandment is, Jesus replied to the young man, "'You shall love the Lord your God with all your heart, and with all your soul, and with all your mind' And a second is like it: 'You shall love your neighbor as yourself.' On these two commandments hang all the law and the prophets" (Mt 22:37-40). Here, Jesus summarizes the entire Law by singling out specific two commands: the love of God (Dt 6:5) and love of neighbor (Lv 19:18). In doing so, he is telling us that God loves us and wants us to join him in spreading God's love by participating in his divine life and actions. Through Baptism, we are immersed in Christ's Paschal Mystery and become members of his Mystical Body. This corporate person is both human and divine. By sharing in Christ's humanity, we also become partakers in his divinity. As such, we continue God's creative, redemptive, and sanctifying missions throughout history and down the corridors of time. As Jesus himself said: "All authority in heaven and on earth has been given to me. Go therefore and make disciples of all nations, baptizing them in the name of the Father and the Son and the Holy Spirit, and teaching them to obey everything that I have commanded you. And remember, I am with you always, to the end of the age" (Mt 28:18-20).

Chapter One: The Origins of Mission

A Christian Anthropology of Mission

Our call to mission flows from God's own heart and involves both being and action. Because of this, and since we are created in his image and likeness, our mission flows necessarily from our own being and actions. To understand this call to mission, therefore, it is necessary for us to understand the various dimensions of our human makeup: the physical, intellectual/psychological, spiritual, and communal. To neglect any one of these dimensions would be to fall short of the full implications of the mission to which we are called. Needless to say, these dimensions are all intimately related.

The Physical. Unlike the many dualistic, heretical movements of the past (e.g. Gnosticism, Manichaeism, Catharism, and some of today's New Age spiritualities), Christianity affirms the fundamental goodness of the material world. At the same time, it holds that the world God created has fallen from the path originally ordained by him and that the human race, the pinnacle of God's creation because it has been endowed with reason and free will, has played a major role in this fall from grace. The Catholic doctrine of original sin states that the account of the Fall in Genesis 3 is a figurative depiction of a primeval event that occurred at the dawn of human history.[1] It tells us that we sense in the depths of our consciousness that the world we live in is not how God had originally intended it to be and that we share some (if not all) responsibility for our current situation.

If God's creative action has somehow gone awry, his redeeming action has made it right by the Incarnation, Passion, Death, and Resurrection of Jesus Christ, and the sanctifying work of the Holy Spirit, who ever since has made the fruits of Christ's Redemptive action manifest in our world. Because we are made in the image and likeness of God and are called to share in an intimate friendship with Our Lord, we are also called to share in God's re-creation of the fallen world by playing a role in His ongoing creative, redemptive, and sanctifying actions. What does this mean concretely?

First and foremost, it means we must care for God's creation, cultivate it rather than exploit it, and be good stewards of all that God has given us. Once we realize that God created the world we live in so we

---

[1] See *Catechism of the Catholic Church*, no. 390.

could freely live in fellowship with him and that he has given it to us so that, with his continuing help, we could nurture it, help it to grow, and ultimately transform it, we look upon it in an entirely different light. When seen through the lens of our participation in God's creative, redemptive, and sanctifying actions, it means that we should look upon the world around us as a gift from God to be appreciated, cared for, and fostered. Rather than being pitted against it so that we could consume and capitalize on it for our own selfish ends, we should look upon ourselves as that part of God's creation that has been specifically tasked to watch over its ongoing well-being.

In the second place, it means we should look upon our own physical existence as an intimate part of our identity of being, which we are called to care for rather than abuse, nurture rather than disdain. For this reason, we are called to foster our physical health by eating and drinking well, getting enough sleep and physical exercise, going for regular medical checkups, and doing everything necessary to keep the corporeal dimension of our lives in sync with the other dimensions of our human makeup. What is more, it means we should take the time to immerse ourselves in the beauty of God's creation rather than isolating ourselves in the concrete jungles of today's modern cities. The more we separate our corporeal being from the Creation's natural beauty, the more we will tend to view it as something to be conquered and exploited rather than cultivated and care for.

Finally, we should not only care for and nurture our own corporeal existence, but we should also look after the physical well-being of those around us. Catholic teaching places the corporal works of mercy at the heart of what it means to love others as we love ourselves. We are called by God to feed the hungry, give drink to the thirsty, clothe the naked, shelter the homeless, care for the sick, visit the imprisoned, and bury the dead.[2] Those we live with should be cared for, rather than looked upon as threats or competitors or, even worse, simply ignored. The human race is an integral part of God's creation, and we have a special call to care for the physical well-being of the poor and vulnerable, the sick and vulnerable, those who, for whatever reason, find themselves homeless and unable to care for themselves.

---

[2] See *Catechism of the Catholic Church*, nos. 2447-48.

The Intellectual/Psychological. We are, however, more than just physical beings. There is an interior aspect of our human identity. We have reason that enables us to think, a will that gives direction to our actions, and feelings that allow our interior world to react to the world around us. There is also a subconscious dimension to our lives that puts us in touch with our deeper selves, one that affects our thoughts and actions, our memory and imagination, in ways of which we are barely aware.

Because of our original fall from grace, this intellectual/psychological dimension of our lives is less than what it was originally intended to be. The sin of our first parents darkened our minds, weakened our wills, and placed our feelings and emotions out of sync with each other, as well as with our higher intellectual faculties. We now live in a darkened, sinful world, where even our memory and imagination take us to places we would rather not go. Jesus came to heal these badly warped aspects of our lives—and even transform them. Like us in all things but sin, he conquered death by means of his passion, death, and resurrection and, as a result, healed us of these deep intellectual/psychological wounds. He became human so that we might become divine.[3] Whether that becomes a reality in our lives depends to the extent to which we are willing to cooperate with His transforming grace.

Because we are created in God's image and likeness, we are called to spread the Good News of Christ's saving and transforming power to every dimension of our human makeup. That goes even for the levels of mind, will, memory, imagination, and feeling. Christ came to heal us but, unlike the Evil One, he refuses do so against our will. For him to heal us of the broken intellectual/psychological aspects of our lives, we must allow him in. When seen in this light, our mission to this dimension of our lives is to let go of ourselves so that Christ can work his wonders within us.

The old saying in the Catholic tradition, "grace perfects nature,"[4] is relevant here. Christ's grace does not destroy these weakened aspects of our interior lives but heals and transforms them from within. He

---

[3] See Athanasius of Alexandria, *On the Incarnation*, 54.3.

[4] See Thomas Aquinas, *Summa theologiae*, I, q. 1, a. 8, ad 2m.

Chapter One: The Origins of Mission   15

does so by infusing into our lives the theological virtues of faith, hope, and charity so that they redirect our natural virtues of prudence, justice, fortitude, and temperance to God by becoming grace-filled and focused entirely on him. Prudence, which seeks appropriate rational means to achieve ends in accord with human nature, now seeks those ways that will best lead us to God. Justice, which naturally seeks to give each person his or her due, seeks to give God His due and what everyone else is due in the eyes of God. Fortitude, which tames our irascible appetite and knows when to retreat and when to attack in the face of danger, now views such dangers in the light of our eternal destiny and inspires to lay down our lives in ways both large and small to achieve that end. Temperance, which tames our concupiscible appetite and seeks moderation in all things, now enables us to view everything we consume in the light of God's desire to befriend us and live in our hearts.

When all is said and done, it is the grace of the Spirit that redirects our minds, will, memory, imagination, and feelings to live under the gentle rule of reason's reign. Jesus, we must remember, is the Logos, the Word-made-flesh, the Eternal Wisdom of the

Father. His Spirit seeks to transform the intellectual/psychological aspects of our human makeup and fill them with his myriad gifts and fruits. Those gifts are "wisdom, understanding, counsel, fortitude, knowledge, piety, and fear of the Lord."[5] And the fruits of the Spirit are "charity, joy, peace, patience, kindness, goodness, generosity, gentleness, faithfulness, modesty, self-control, and chastity."[6] These gifts and fruits imbue the intellectual/psychological aspects of our being and direct our paths to God.

The Spiritual. Still, we are more than physical and intellectual/psychological beings. There is also a spiritual dimension to our human makeup. The Apostle Paul writes, "May the God of peace himself sanctify you entirely; and may your spirit and soul and body be kept sound and blameless at the coming of our Lord Jesus Christ" (1Th 5:23). What exactly do we mean by "spirit," and how can we differentiate it from the soul and body? The human spirit is the deepest dimension of the human person. It is that aspect of our nature that yearns for God and can enter into

---

[5] See *Catechism of the Catholic Church*, no. 1830-31.
[6] See *Catechism of the Catholic Church*, no. 1832.

communion with Him. It is deeper than human thought and volition and has no need of memory or imagination. It is a secret longing for God deep within us that can be filled by no other person or thing but God Himself.

As St. Paul reminds us, "We know that the whole creation has been groaning in labor pains until now; and not only the creation, but we ourselves, who have the first fruits of the Spirit, groan inwardly while we wait for adoption, the redemption of our bodies" (Rom 8:22-23). A little later, he remarks, "Likewise the Spirit helps us in our weakness; for we do not know how to pray as we ought, but that very Spirit intercedes with sighs too deep for words" (Rom 8:26). The human spirit is the place within us that communes with the Holy Spirit, whose myriad gifts and fruits overflow from there into the other dimensions of our being. St. Augustine of Hippo says it best, "You stir man to take pleasure in praising you, because you have made us for yourself, and our heart is restless until it rests in you."[7] This "Holy Longing," as Ronald Rolheiser describes us, accompanies us throughout

---

[7] Augustine of Hippo, *Confessions* 1.1.

our lives.[8] It may be blunted or weakened by the way we live our lives, but it can never be extinguished. It is a fundamental element of our human makeup and comprises the basis of what St. Paul calls the "new self" as opposed to the "old self" (Eph 4:22-24).

It is important for us to remember that the dimensions of our human makeup do not exist apart from each other but are intimately related. They are not separate "parts" that can be isolated and examined independently from one another. To do so would be an insult to our Creator in whose image and likeness we have been made and who sustains us in existence "drop by drop" (*guttatim*), from one moment to the next. Just as God is One-yet-Many by virtue of the Three relations of love within Him, so, too, are we one in our physical, intellectual/psychological, spiritual, and social dimensions, but also many since these dimensions of our being relate to one another in distinct ways. This holds true especially for the spiritual.

The spiritual dimension of our lives is that area where the Holy Spirit longs within us and continually

---

[8] See Ronald Rolheiser, *The Holy Longing: The Search for Christian Spirituality* (New York: Doubleday, 1999).

groans for God. As St. Paul says, "When we cry, 'Abba! Father!' it is that very Spirit bearing witness with our spirit that we are children of God, and if children, then heirs, heirs of God and joint heirs with Christ—if, in fact, we suffer with him so that we may also be glorified with him" (Rom 8:15-17). The presence of the Spirit in our lives reminds us that we are adopted sons and daughters of the Father. What is more, because love itself is freely self-diffusive, the Spirit who communes with our spirit in the very depths of our being overflows into the other dimensions of our makeup, suffers with us as we journey through life, and glorifies us as the Son was glorified. The Spirit, in other words, overflows from our spirit into our minds, our bodies, and will one day raise us up to share the resurrected and glorified existence of Christ's Mystical Body. This overflow (*redundantia*) of the Spirit into our lives will put us in touch with Jesus' glorified humanity and enables us to share in the intimate love of the Trinity.

The Communal. We are also social, communal beings. We were born to live together, as a family, in a parish, a community, a country, and nation. Without the experience of this communal dimension of our human makeup, we would never become our truest, deepest selves. There is the story of two scientists who wanted to discover the original human language. They took a newborn child from an orphanage that kept him locked up in a room. For much of his early life, he was provided with all the basic necessities: food, water, shelter, clothing. From the moment he was placed in isolation, he had no contact whatsoever with another human being. All the necessities were placed in his room at night when he was asleep. When he reached adolescence, the scientists made the first human contact he had ever had since he was born. Much to their chagrin, when they tried to communicate with him, he spoke nothing but gibberish. They found that there was no original human language, but it is learned from others, by living in human society. Without any access to human culture, we have no way of communicating with others. By living with others, we learn how to communicate with them either by way of words, signs, expressions, or what have you. Without human contact, we can easily devolve into our animal natures. The stories of how infants raised by wild animals (e.g., a pack of wolves) take on the characteristics of those who rear them bears this out.

Such stories may or may not be true. The point they are making, however, is that we were born to be in relationship with others. We are born this way because we are created in the image and likeness of the God, who Himself is a relation being: Three Divine Persons in One God. What is more, even the child raised in isolation or by a pack of wild wolves never loses his or her humanity. Once introduced into human society, their capacity to relate to others is reawakened, and they begin the long process of learning how to live in human society. The reason for this is natural law that is imprinted in our hearts and shapes human behavior according to certain truths: do good and avoid evil; self-preservation, procreation and the education of offspring, life in a just society. Such laws or principles are deeply embedded in our hearts and set us apart from the rest of creation since they represent a participation or sharing in the Eternal Law, the Logos of God Himself, the Second Person of the Blessed Trinity, who became incarnate in the Person of Jesus of Nazareth, the one we refer to as the Christ. While the more derivative human laws move away from these first principles of natural law, the less certainty we can have about their validity, yet it remains true that, as beings created in the image and likeness of God, we have certain basic principles embedded in our hearts that, once their meaning become clear, we instinctively know to be true and seek to implement in our lives.[9]

Besides natural law, the social dimension of our human makeup is also affirmed in Sacred Scripture. We have already seen that God has called each of us to share in a relationship of intimate friendship with him. He loves us so much that he wants to share his divinity with us. It is ironic that what tempted Adam and Eve in the Garden (to "be like God" [Gen 3:5]) was in God's plan all along. The difference is that our first parents tried to seize it for themselves rather than accepting it as a part of God's plan for them. In

---

[9] For the classical treatment of natural law theory in the Catholic tradition, see Thomas Aquinas, *Summa theologiae*, I-II, q.94, aa. 1-6. For a contemporary treatment, see The International Theological Commission, *In Search of a Universal Ethic: A New Look at Natural Law* (2009), https://www.vatican.va/roman_curia/congregations/cfaith/cti_documents/rc_con_cfaith_doc_20090520_legge-naturale_en.html (accessed August 13, 2025).

the New Testament, St. Paul highlights the social nature of our human makeup and places it in the context of being members of Christ's body:

> "For just as the body is one and has many members, and all the members of the body, though many, are one body, so it is with Christ. For in the one Spirit we were all baptized into one body—Jews or Greeks, slaves or free—and we were all made to drink of the one Spirit. Indeed, the body does not consist of one member but of many. If the foot would say, "Because I am not a hand, I do not belong to the body," that would not make it any less a part of the body. And if the ear would say, "Because I am not an eye, I do not belong to the body," that would not make it any less a part of the body. If the whole body were an eye, where would the hearing be? If the whole body were hearing, where would the sense of smell be? But as it is, god arranged the embers in the body, each one of them, as he chose. If all were a single member, where would the body be? As it is, there are many members, yet one body." (1 Cor 12:12-20)

The body of Christ is not a simple image or metaphor but points to a transcendent reality known as the Mystical Body of Christ. It points to the belief that, as members of Christ's body, we already have a share in His glorified, resurrected humanity and are one day destined to partake of its fulness.

Conclusion

Christian mission flows from God's nature and the relations within him that form an intimate community of divine love. The phrase, "God is love" (1 Jn 4:8) captures the very essence of God and, since love must express itself to some other, it follows that multiple relations exist within the one divine nature. The doctrine of the Trinity embodies this truth by stating that there are Three Persons in one God. Each Person shares in the one divine substance and is differentiated from the others by the nature of its relationship to them. The Father *generates*; the Son *returns* that love by uniting his will the Father; the Spirit, in turn, *proceeds* from the mutual love of the Father and his Son.

Since love is self-diffusive, God voluntarily expresses his love beyond himself through three eternal actions: Creation, Redemption, and Sanctification.

Although God always acts as one, each of these acts is typically associated with one of the three divine Persons: Creation with the Father, Redemption with the Son, and Sanctification with the Holy Spirit. God diffuses his love through these three divine actions. What is more, since God created us in this image and likeness, it follows that we were made for love and that, like him, we are called to diffuse that love freely through similar actions. That is to say that God loves us so much that he wants us to share in his creative, redemptive, and sanctifying activity. As mentioned earlier, he became human so we might become divine.

Because we are created in God's image and likeness, the Christian mission flows from our very being. It must embrace every aspect of our human makeup: physical, intellectual/psychological, spiritual, and communal. We cannot give to others what we ourselves do not have. Our actions in this mission flow from God's immeasurable love for us and extends first to ourselves, then to others, and ultimately to all creation. We are called to bring Christ's love to this moment in space and time where we find ourselves. He came to bring about a new Creation and does so not by destroying the old but by transforming it from within. When seen in this light, the origins of Christianity are in God himself and his desire for us to accompany him in his divine activity.

Chapter Two

Mission in St. Alphonsus

Having considered the origins of Christian mission in general, we can now look at its more specific origins in the life of St. Alphonsus de Liguori (1696-1787), the founder of the Redemptorist Congregation. By gaining some insight into what motivated him to reach out to the poor and most abandoned peasants and sheepherders in the remote hilltop villages and countryside of southern Italy, we will be able to set the context for the larger Redemptorist mission to the wider world. Only by looking to the spirit of their founder will today's Redemptorists and their larger family be able to discern their missionary call in today's world. Not to do so would be a disservice to their history and missionary heritage. We begin by looking at Alphonsus's early life and the circumstances that led him to his daring missionary outreach.

Alphonsus's Missionary Outlook

Alphonsus Maria de Liguori was born at Marianella on the outskirts of Naples into a deeply religious family of the lower Neapolitan nobility. His father was a captain in the Royal Navy, and his mother a pious woman who took great care to give her eight children a strong foundation in the Catholic faith. Being the eldest of the children and heir apparent to the family legacy, Alphonsus was expected by his father to climb the social hierarchy and promote the family's interests in the kingdom. To this end, he was tutored at home in literature, music, and the arts, enrolled in the University of Naples at a young age, and earned a doctorate in both canon and civil law at the age of sixteen. In the following decade, Alphonsus set out on a highly successful career in law that was later shattered in his loss of a highly contentious lawsuit due to bribery and political interference. This loss threw Alphonsus into a deep depression, one that triggered some deep, existential soul-searching regarding his true purpose in life. After days alone and of cutting himself off from family and friends, he found himself visiting some of the nearby churches of Naples and eventually in the Church of Our Lady of Ransom. After the service, he went to the altar of Our Lady of Mercy, drew his nobleman's sword, placed it at Our Lady's feet, and promised to pursue a vocation to the priesthood.

Up to this point, Alphonsus's life had already been shaped by holy exercises that fostered in him a deep desire to bring aid to and comfort the poor. In addition to attending Mass and spiritual devotions such as Eucharistic adoration and Forty Hours, he attended with his father regular retreats for men with the Vincentians, Oratorians, and Jesuits. What is more, he sought to put his faith in action by bringing food and comfort to the patients of the Hospital of the Incurables in Naples. This desire to live out his faith was present at an early age and reached maturity in his decision to become a priest. Persuaded by his father not to enter a religious order, Alphonsus became a diocesan priest of the Archdiocese of Naples and eventually took up residence in the Chinese College in Naples and became a member of the priestly confraternity known as the Apostolic Missions. During this time, his missionary outreach was focused mainly to evangelizing the poor people of Naples (*lazzaroni*) through evening street preaching and catechesis known as the Evening Chapels (*Cappelle Serotine*). Alphonsus's preaching was simple and easy to understand. He believed that each of his hearers should be able to understand his message. The Gospel, in his mind, should be accessible to all, and he was thoroughly against any preacher's efforts to be learned and sophisticated.

In his years as a diocesan priest, Alphonsus dedicated himself tirelessly to the preaching the Gospel to the people of Naples. Although there was no shortage of priests in the kingdom, most were hesitant to go to the remote country villages that made up the major portion of the geographic landscape of the kingdom. This became abundantly clear to him when he went on retreat to Scala, a small town on the Amalfi coast, to rest from his intensive preaching engagements. Staying at the Casa Anastasio, on the rural outskirts of the town, he was struck by the lack of spiritual care available to the people of the area, most of whom were poor farmers and sheepherders. This encounter sowed in his heart a desire reach-out to those in the remote places of the kingdom who had seemly been abandoned by the Church. It was from this inspiration that Alphonsus founded the Congregation of the Most Holy Savior, later to be known as the Congregation of the most Holy Redeemer, popularly known as the Redemptorists.[1]

Alphonsus's Overall Missionary Strategy

If the origins of Alphonsus's missionary zeal flowed from his own conversion of heart and personal zeal for bringing the Gospel to those on the margins of society, his missionary strategy for implementing this goal of evangelizing the poor and most abandoned stemmed from his assessment of the needs of these people and his decision to bring the Good News of plentiful redemption to them, rather than having them come to him and his fellow missionaries.

---

[1] For more on St. Alphonsus and the founding of the Redemptorists, see Frederick M. Jones, *Alphonsus de Liguori: The Saint of Bourbon Naples (1696-1787)* (Dublin: Gill and MacMillan, 1992), 90-110; Théodule Rey-Mermet, *St. Alphonsus: Tireless Worker for the Most Abandoned*, trans. Jehanne-Marie Marchesi (Brooklyn, NY; New City Press, 1987), 257-506.

Alphonsus's overall missionary strategy was influenced by his understanding of the underlying Gospel message he was called to proclaim: God entered our world in the mystery of the Incarnation (Crib), gave himself completely to us by his suffering and death on the cross (Cross), became a source of nourishment for us in the Eucharist (Sacrament), and a source of hope for us in his Resurrection and Ascension into heaven (Mary). Mary, "our life, our sweetness, and our hope," represents the fullness of this hope, since she has been assumed bodily into heaven, shares fully in his glorified humanity, and experiences this very moment the fullness of redemption. Taking this Gospel narrative to heart, Alphonsus sought to replicate it in his own life and the lives of his followers. He sought to enter the world of the people he was called to serve, give himself completely to them, become a source of nourishment for them, and a source of hope for them. After all, Jesus himself said, "If any want to become my followers, let them deny themselves and take up their cross daily and follow me" (Lk 9:23). Alphonsus wanted his Redemptorist missionaries to be "other christs" to the people they served. They were to do so by bringing the presence of Christ in their midst and introducing them to God's desire to befriend them, dwell in their hearts, so they might live in his. Alphonsus's overall missionary strategy was to bring Christ's presence to the people they served. This presence alone would liberate them from the chains of sin that had enslaved them ever since the story of the Fall and the sin of our first parents.

Also underlying his overall strategy was the sacramental nature of Catholicism, which affirmed God's use of Creation (e.g., water, oil, bread and wine) to bring the paschal mystery to God's people down the corridors of time to mediate his saving redemptive grace. The seven sacraments, Baptism, Confirmation, Eucharist, Penance, Matrimony, Orders, and Anointing of the Sick, were outward signs instituted by Christ that immersed God's people in the mystery of Redemption and, in accordance, were meant to be distributed in accordance with the customs of the times. Alphonsus considered those who were deprived of these life-giving mysteries as people overlooked and, at times, even abandoned by the Church's pastors. What is more, the people in these marginal areas were often poorly educated, illiterate, and lacking even the most basic rudiments of the faith. Alphonsus witnessed this need firsthand when he ventured to the impoverished hill country south of Naples and committed himself and, later, his fellow Redemptorists to fill that gap as much as possible.

Taken together, these aspects of Alphonsus's missionary strategy—Word (Gospel narrative) and Sacrament—underscore the immediacy of God's invitation to open their hearts, repent, and receive in their hearts his forgiveness and redeeming grace. They underscore the underlying Catholic warp and woof of his missionary endeavors and God's generous offer of plentiful redemption to everyone who has ears to hear. The Redemptorist motto, "With him is plentiful redemption" (*Copiosa apud eum redemptio*), encapsulates the meaning of Alphonsus's whole missionary strategy. In an age that was haunted by Jansenist rigorism, on the one hand, and moral laxism, on the other, Alphonsus brought to the people of his day an interpretation of the Gospel that was sensitive to the demands of the Law yet rooted in God's mercy and forgiveness. His overall missionary strategy was intended to bring Christ's Gospel message to those most in need of hearing it: the poor and abandoned.

Jesus himself said he came to fulfill these words of the prophet Isaiah, "The Spirit of the Lord is upon me, because he has anointed me to bring good news to the poor. He has sent me to proclaim release to the captives and recovery of sight to the blind, to let the oppressed go free, to proclaim the year of the Lord's favor" (Lk 4:18-19). In their day, Alphonsus and his fellow Redemptorists sought to proclaim Jesus' message anew in their little corner of the world to anyone willing to listen.

Alphonsus's Concrete Missionary Strategy

Before he founded the Redemptorists, Alphonsus was already a seasoned mission preacher through his work with the Apostolic Missions, which focused primarily on evangelizing the poor in urban areas. His inspiration to evangelize the poor in rural areas of the kingdom was partly inspired by Bishop Thomas Falcoia (d 1749), who for many years also served as Alphonsus's spiritual director. Falcoia was a member of the Congregation of Pious Workers, as well as a seasoned mission preacher. Both he and

Alphonsus were familiar with the established mission system and initiated some fundamental changes.

To begin with, Alphonsus changed the idea of a central mission. Rather than going out to the outlying towns and villages of the area, the traditional mission chose a central location from which the missioners preached, and people were asked to travel there. In many cases, this travel inconvenience discouraged many from going, possibly even those who needed to hear the message of God's merciful love for them the most. Alphonsus, instead, wanted the Redemptorists to go to those distant and inaccessible rural areas to share the Good News. Their arrival in these localities was often a cause of celebration since many in these places felt forgotten by the Church and were delighted to see someone willing to go out of their way to visit them, teach them, administer the sacraments to them and, in a special way, hear their confessions. This innovation proved to be highly successful, for it brought hope to the inhabitants of these distant rural towns and villages, encouraged them, and renewed their faith.

The second innovation made by Alphonsus was to expand the time allotted for the mission, which up

Chapter Two: Mission in St. Alphonsus

until then had been relatively short and inadequate for meeting the spiritual needs of the people. Alphonsus extended the time of the mission thus allowing more time and space for hearing confessions, teaching the faith, visiting the sick, and administering the last rites. These missions lasted for roughly two weeks and were often supplemented with follow-up renewal visits some months later. The purpose of these visits was to confirm the people in their faith and to encourage them to continue practicing their faith through the prayers and devotions they had been taught. These holy exercises (mental prayer, adoration, visits to the Blessed Sacrament, the rosary, novenas, etc.) were meant to keep the faith of these poor peasant farmers and sheep herders alive in the absence of the Church's sacramental ministry.

A third innovation that Alphonsus brought to the popular mission was to simplify the style of preaching. In his day, preachers were often known to employ a florid style that showboated the learning and sophistication of the preacher rather than the childlike simplicity of the Gospel message. This approach had many disadvantages. For one thing, it made their message inaccessible to the less educated, who could neither follow the highly constructed sentence structure nor the various references to classical literature and learned figures being made. What is more, it placed the preacher before the message and therefore made it difficult for the Spirit to penetrate the hearts of the faithful and bring about the fundamental conversion (*metanoia*) that was the primary purpose for have the mission in the first place. Finally, it heightened the social distinctions within the congregation, since only those who understood what was said could discuss it later, and only with their peers. Alphonsus was thoroughly against this style of preaching. He insisted that Redemptorist preachers spoke in a simple style that everyone in the congregation, both the learned and the uneducated faithful, could understand. Such simplicity in preaching placed the Gospel message before the preacher and became a hallmark of the Redemptorist style.

In the fourth place, Alphonsus also emphasized the importance of the missioner having a simple lifestyle. He understood that the words the missioner would wane insignificance if they were not backed up by a style of living that itself proclaimed the truth of the Gospel message. Preachers who say one thing but do not back up their words by their actions are rarely effective custodians of God's Word and may even hinder it spread. For this reason, they should dress simply, eat and drink simple fare, avoid luxurious pastimes, and associate with all types of people, not just the rich and famous or those well-positioned in society. The Redemptorist reputation of being "kitchen priests" flows from this requirement of the Redemptorist mission preacher. People should feel free to welcome them into their homes without having to put up a fuss about how to treat or welcome them. Their lifestyle should reflect that of Jesus and his disciples, who went about the countryside of Judea and Galilee without caring about where they would stay or what they would eat. God would take care of them, they believed, and would never abandon them.

Finally, Alphonsus emphasized the community dimension of the Redemptorist mission. He viewed the Redemptorist missionary project as fundamentally communal in nature. That is to say that they were called to live together in community and given witness to the Gospel message by their simplicity of life and the witness they gave to others through their life in community. This communitarian dimension of the Redemptorist mission was essential to their efforts. Individual Redemptorists lived their lives through their communities. They shared what they earned, lived off the common table, and shared what little they had with those in need. In this way, they reflected the communal lifestyle of the earliest Christian communities which, as we are told in the Acts of the Apostles, shared everything in common (Acts 4:32). Alphonsus wanted the Redemptorists to reflect this apostolic lifestyle in their own lives and believed it would be a means through which they could spread the Gospel message.[2]

These five characteristics of the Redemptorist mission—outreach to the marginalized, being present to them, simplicity of preaching, an unassuming lifestyle, and a focused stress on community—are fundamental elements of the Redemptorist charism and remain so to this day. Although, interpretations

---

[2] The above five characteristics of Alphonsus's missionary strategy come from Joseph W. Oppitz, *Alphonsian History and Spirituality: A Study of the Spirit of the Founder, St. Alphonsus M. Liguori and of the Missionary Institute, the Missionary Institute, The Congregation of the Most Holy Redeemer* (ad usum privatum), 32-33.

of what they might mean for Redemptorists in their particular time and locality may vary to some degree, confreres from all over the world should affirm these values and live them out to the best of their ability.

Implications of Alphonsus's Missionary Strategy

This now brings us to the question of how today's Redemptorists should implement Alphonsus's missionary strategy. To do so we must avoid two extremes: (1) Trying to implement Alphonsus's strategy as it is, word for word, without allowing room for adapting it to different national and cultural situations and (2) thinking that the Redemptorist world has changed so much its nearly 300-year history that it has almost nothing to say to the present needs and concerns of today's world. Neither could be further from the truth. The need to preach the Gospel to the poor and most abandoned is a concern for Christians of all ages. While considerations to changing times and cultural milieus must be considered, Alphonsus's missionary insights still have much to offer us today. What follows is at least a partial list of what these considerations might include.

Watchfulness. Redemptorists and members the wider Redemptorist family should be alert to situations of poverty and abandonment in the world around them. Alphonsus went to Scala on retreat and found there a pastoral need that touched him deeply and motivated him to do something about it. In a similar manner, today's Redemptorists should be aware of the world around them and willing to move out of their comfort zones rather than staying in safe and well-tried ministries that have grown as a result of their efforts and no longer have great need of their presence.

Approachable. Redemptorists, moreover, should also make great efforts to be present and approachable to those they serve. Rather than coming across as distant and foreign, they should strive to meet them where they are and encourage them to take the next necessary steps for their growth in holiness. This means being able to talk to them on their level rather than talking down to them. It also means being willing to listen to lay out their problems and difficulties, as well as their concerns about their family, relatives, and friends. Redemptorists should be "kitchen priests" at all times and in every sense of the phrase.

Adaptable. Redemptorists should also seek to be faithful to Alphonsus's insights, yet also willing to adapt his vision to the exigences of their present ministerial circumstances. This means being willing to discern the pastoral needs of the faithful around them and minister to them even if it was not in Alphonsus's original plan for the Congregation. St. Clement Hofbauer's willingness to take on the pastoral needs of St. Beno's parish in Poland and turning it into what amounted to a perpetual mission is one such example of their being able to adapt Alphonsus's missionary vision to the needs and exigencies at hand.

Mobile. Whatever pastoral ministry Redemptorists find themselves in, as true missionaries they should be willing to go where needed and not be tied down to any particular place because of history, tradition, or a call by the congregation to minister elsewhere. While careful, prudent discernment is called for in such situations, and while they must have a high regard for their Redemptorist past, they must not permit it to become the sole matrix that governs their decisions. They must respect the past, live in the present, and be sensitive to where the Lord is presently calling them as a Congregation, as individual Provinces, local communities, and individuals. Otherwise, they will eventually become mere relics of the past with little or no relevance to present needs of the faithful.

Self-Evaluating. Alphonsus saw the importance of having regular meetings on the local level to look at particular case studies that would help the confreres better their ministry in the confessional and have experienced confreres train them in the finer details of mission preaching and catechesis. In a similar way, Redemptorists today should not be afraid to look at how their ministries are progressing, evaluate them, and be willing to change course when needed. They need to do this as individuals, in their local communities, in their Provinces, and in the world-wide Congregation. Without this element of self-reflection, their ministries can easily become stagnant, lifeless, and unengaging

Prayerful. Alphonsus called prayer "the great means of salvation." It is the means through which grace penetrates our lives, both communally and personally, to help them make our way toward God. For this reason, Redemptorists must look upon prayer, both personal and liturgical, as a foundational element of their spiritual and missionary lives, rather than an accidental add-on disconnected from the rest of life. Without prayer, their missionary spirit will soon grow cold, and their ministries become empty of spirit and vitality. With prayer, they can do all things, "For nothing will be impossible with God" (Lk 1:37).

Communal. Redemptorists must also constantly keep in mind that Alphonsus placed great value on community life. This means living together, eating together, meeting for set times for prayer, recreating together, and meeting regularly to discuss the ministries they are engaged in. This should be done both on the local and Provincial levels. Care should also be taken to invite our Partners in Mission to various gatherings for purposes of getting to know them better and possibly sharing our missions with them.

These are but a few of the areas where Alphonsus's missionary strategy can be adapted and employed by Redemptorists today. All members of the Redemptorist family, priests, brothers, and lay, should strive to embody these qualities in their daily lives and promote them as best they can in all they do.

Conclusion

Alphonsus's missionary outlook flowed from his own conversion of heart and desire to bring the love of Christ to others. His disillusionment with the world as a result of his loss of an important legal case due to bribery and political interference caused him to reevaluate the direction his life was taking and culminated in his bold decision against his father's will to become a Catholic priest. His concern for others was already apparent as a layman in his ministry to the sick at the Hospital of the Incurables and, after his ordination, in his preaching the Evening Chapels (*Capelle Serotine*) in the poor ghetto areas of Naples and as a mission preacher for the Apostolic Missions in Naples. His experience of how spiritually neglected the poor were in the rural areas of the kingdom led him to found the Redemptorist Congregation.

Alphonsus's overall missionary strategy has its roots in his understanding of the underlying narrative of the Gospel message and the sacramental nature of the Church. His approach to the evangelization of the poor was to bring both Word and Sacrament to them so that God's healing and transforming grace could enter their hearts and bring about a radical conversion. To accomplish this end, he decentralized the currently accepted plan of the traditional mission and brought the Gospel message to the people rather than having them come to him. He also extended the time of the mission and had follow-up renewals so that there would be ample time to be present the people, preach God's word, hear their confessions, and visit the sick. What is more, he simplified the style of the mission sermon, insisted that the preachers reflect Gospel values in their lifestyle, and emphasized the importance of community in the life of his fledgling missionary congregation.

These elements of Alphonsus's missionary strategy have great relevance for today's Redemptorists and their wider spiritual family. It reminds them that they are to be "priests of the people" rather than "above the people." It also asks them to be watchful, approachable, adaptable, mobile, self-adjusting, prayerful, and communal in the way they deal with others and conduct their missionary efforts. They are to be "other christs" to those they serve in their concrete historical circumstances. The purpose of all this is to ensure that Christ's plentiful redemption was proclaimed to everyone, so he may live in their hearts—and they in his.

Chapter Three

Preaching the Gospel

Now that we have explored the origins of the concept of "Mission" itself and Alphonsus's understanding of it, we can look at what preaching the Gospel meant to St. Alphonsus and its relevance for us today. We shall examine his treatment of this subject in a number of his writings and in a document on preaching produced by one of the early Redemptorist chapters. The goal here is to affirm the importance of a simple style rooted in Gospel values that emphasizes the centrality of God's grace in bringing about fundamental conversion (*metanoia*).

St. Alphonsus on Preaching

Preaching the Gospel was at the heart at Alphonsus's understanding of mission. As he says in the *Selva: Dignity and Duties of the Priest*, "By preaching, the faith has been promulgated, and by the same means God wishes it to be preserved: 'So faith comes through what is heard, and what is heard comes through the word of Christ' (Rom 10:17)."[1] Let us take a look at four key documents that underscore the important emphasis Alphonsus places on the ministry on preaching in Christ's Church: *Constitution on Preaching* (1747),[2] *Selva* (1760), *Letter to a Religious on the Maner of Preaching* (1761),[3] and *Refutation of a French Book Entitled,* On Preaching (1767).[4] Each on its own way underscores the tremendous privilege

---

[1] Alphonsus de Liguori, *Selva, Dignity and Duties of the Priest*, ed. Eugene Grimm, The Complete Works of Saint Alphonsus de Liguori, vol. 12 (Brooklyn: Redemptorist Fathers, 1927), 265. [Some words have been translated into modern English].

[2] See Carl Hoegerl, *Founding Texts of Redemptorist Early Rules and Allied Documents* (Rome: Collegio Sant' Alfonso, 1986), 61-247. The historical background of this document comes from this source.

[3] Alphonsus de Liguori, *Letter to a Religious on the Manner of Preaching,* ed. Eugene Grimm, The Complete Works of Saint Alphonsus de Liguori, vol. 15 (Brooklyn: Redemptorist Fathers, 1890), 17-62. [Some words have been translated into modern English].

[4] Alphonsus de Liguori, *Refutation of a French Book Entitled on Preaching* ed. Eugene Grimm, The Complete Works of Saint Alphonsus de Liguori, vol. 15 (Brooklyn: Redemptorist Fathers, 1890) 63-72. [Some words have been translated into modern English].

and responsibility those have who have been entrusted by Christ and his Church with the proclamation of God's Word.

Constitution on Preaching. This relatively brief document came from the General Chapter of 1747. Alphonsus was Rector Major at the time and, no doubt, had an important hand in its drafting. Although it does not appear in the *Acta* and was likely not brought to the floor, it was signed by the Chapter Secretary and represents one of the earliest Redemptorist documents that specifically discusses the role of preaching within the Congregation and, with some slight changes and additions, was eventually incorporated into the Constitutions of 1764.

The document begins by quoting the Apostle Paul: "Faith comes through hearing" (Rom 10:17) and "How can they hear unless there is someone to preach" (Rom 10:14). It goes on to say, quoting the Apostle once more when he says, "My message and my preaching had nothing of the persuasive force of 'wise' argumentation, but of the convincing power of the Spirit" (1 Cor 2:4). At the very outset, the document seeks to root Redemptorist preaching in the apostolic tradition by emphasizing the Spirit's power to change hearts and the importance of the preacher to allow the Spirit to speak through him rather than promoting his own talents and the power of 'wise' argumentation."[5]

The *Constitution* goes on to quote notable preachers such as St. John of Avila (1499-1569), St. Francis de Sales (1567-1622) and others, who point out that those who preach out of their own vanity rather than the Spirit are traitors of Jesus Christ, persecutors of the Church, and the reason why many souls are lost. The purpose of preaching, it goes on, is to move the souls of his hearers toward Christ and not to entertain the intellect. It affirms "...that souls do not change their lives with such preaching, because God does not cooperate with vanity."[6]

The remainder of the document states that the members of the Congregation, "...who are especially dedicated to the imitation of Christ and the apostles, and to the care of the poor people in the country, for whom they must chiefly break the bread of the word, are emphatically prohibited to preach with tones, or

---

[5] See Liguori, *Constitution on Preaching*, 342.
[6] Liguori, *Constitution on Preaching*, 342.

vanity of words or ideas."[7] Instead, they are to preach "…in an apostolic manner, without tones; and in a style that is not only clear, simple, familiar (something to be observed in preaching to all classes of people), but also popular when preaching is for the people."[8] Local superiors are specifically charged to monitor each confrere's style of peaching and reprimand those who do not follow the accepted style and choose to do otherwise, even to the point of forbidding those who are obstinate to preach again.[9]

Selva: Dignity and Duties of the Priest. Published in 1760, this work represents the fruit of Alphonsus's many years of missionary work and examines many aspects of priestly life and ministry. In it, he treats the role of preaching in the life of the priest and, in many respects, echoes the insights of the *Constitution on Preaching* treated above. He highlights, for example, the important insight of the Apostle Paul that faith comes through hearing that God's Word must be proclaimed (Rom 10:17). He also calls to mind Paul's words to Timothy: "…proclaim the message; be

---

[7] Liguori, *Constitution on Preaching*, 342-43.

[8] Liguori, *Constitution on Preaching*, 343.

[9] Liguori, *Constitution on Preaching*, 343-44.

consistent whether the time of favorable or unfavorable; convince, rebuke, and encourage, with the utmost patience in teaching" (2 Tim 4:2).

He goes on to say, however, that "...to save souls, it is not enough to preach it is… necessary to preach in a proper manner"[10] "In the first place," he says, "in order to preach well, learning and study are necessary."[11] Preaching at random and without preparation does great harm. To be effective, it is important for the preacher to assimilate God's Word by reading the Scriptures and meditating upon them so that it penetrates the preacher's heart. The preacher must seek to break open the Word, so that it might move from the level of mind to heart. For this reason, the preacher must study what others say about God's Word and how they relate it to other areas of the Church's teaching and ultimately to their own lives. He studies not merely to expand his mind, but also to shape his soul so that it is open to listen to God's Spirit in the depths of his heart and thus be able to preach in the Spirit, and in a way that will move the hearts of his hearers to change their lives.

---

[10] Liguori, *Selva*, 266.
[11] Liguori, *Selva*, 266.

Secondly, Alphonsus states that to save souls, "an exemplary life is necessary."[12] A man who preaches God's Word but does not back it up with his life breeds not love but contempt. People see through his hypocritical ways and do not listen to what he says. Instead, the preacher must allow God's Word to penetrate his heart so that it will bring about a fundamental change in lifestyle, one that emulates the way of life lived by Christ and his disciples. For this to happen, the preacher must have an affection for mental prayer that raises within him the very sentiments he wishes to convey to others: "Mental prayer is the blessed furnace on which sacred orators are inflamed with divine love….Here they form the fiery darts that afterwards wound the hearts of their hearers."[13] What is more, it is necessary to preach not to receive praise or renown, but to do so with the good intention of drawing others to Christ: "He only who speaks from the heart, that is, he who feels and practices what he preaches, shall speak to the hearts of theirs, and shall move them to the love of God."[14] Alphonsus con-

---

[12] Liguori, *Selva*, 266.
[13] Liguori, *Selva*, 267.
[14] Liguori, *Selva*, 267.

cludes, "…it is always expedient to preach in a simple, popular style, not only in the missions and spiritual exercises, but also in all sermons addressed to the people."[15]

Letter to a Religious on the Manner of Preaching. Published in 1761, This work is an extended treatise on the content and manner of preaching that was sent to all the general superiors of religious orders and received high praise for its defense of the importance of simplicity of content, manner, and style when preaching missions, as well as to the faithful in general. It was a response to the criticism of his *Selva* and maintained that "…though sacred orators should preach in a clear and orderly manner, they should never condescend to speak in a popular style; because…such a style is unworthy of the dignity of the pulpit and degrading to the word of God."[16]

Alphonsus viewed this criticism as an opportunity to give an extended defense of his belief that all preaching should be clear, simple, and easy to understand, so that all the preacher's hearers—from the simplest to the most sophisticated—would under-

---

[15] Liguori, *Selva*, 269.
[16] Liguori, *Letter to a Religious*, 17.

stand what was said and could take it to heart. To back up his claims, he quotes from the learned Italian priest, scholar, and important literary critic, Louis Muratori (1672-1750) who, in his popular book, *Popular Eloquence*, promotes Alphonsus's assertion that "…when an audience is composed of the learned and the ignorant, the style of the sermon…should be simple and popular."[17] According to Muratori: "The preacher must speak to the people in the language in which a man of learning would endeavor to persuade a peasant, and thus he will make an impression on the learned as well as on the ignorant."[18]

To back up his claims, Alphonsus also refers to many of the Fathers and Doctors of the Church such as Basil of Caesarea (330-79), Ambrose of Milan, (d. 397), John Chrysostom (d. 407), Augustine of Hippo (354-430), Gregory the Great (d. 604), Thomas Aquinas (1224/5-74) and Bonaventure (1221-4), as well as more recent saints such as Teresa of Avila (1515-82), Philip Neri (1515-95), and St. Francis de Sales (1567-1622). His purpose here is to demonstrate that his position is deeply rooted in the tradition of the

---

[17] Liguori, *Letter to a Religious*,19.
[18] Liguori, *Letter to a Religious*, 22.

Church and that criticisms of him are, in general, criticism of the Church at large. Alphonsus wanted preachers to preach with humility rather than with pride, and simply rather than with sophisticated, ornate speech recognizable to only the learned few. His position can best be summed up in these words:

> "Oh, if all sacred orators preached solely with the view of pleasing God, in an easy and popular style, and discoursed on the truths and the maxims of the Gospel, in a manner plain, simple, and unadorned, and enforced practically the remedies against sins, and the means of persevering and of advancing in the divine love, the world would change its face, and God would not be offended as we now see him. We may remark, that the country parish in which there is a fervent priest, who truly preaches Christ crucified, is soon reclaimed and sanctified, I say, moreover, if a pious and simple discourse is delivered in a church the whole auditory is touched with compunction, and if they are not converted, they are at least moved and affected; if such a style of preaching, then, were

universal, what advantage would we see universally accrue to souls!"[19]

Alphonsus answers his critics both thoroughly and forcefully. His approach is that which brings about the conversion of hearts, which lies at the very heart of what reaching the Gospel is all about.

Refutation of a French Book Entitled, "On Preaching." Soon after his published his *Letter to a Religious on the Manner of Preaching*, Alphonsus came across a work in French that was written by the author the *Philosophical Dictionary*. He found the conclusions of this author so abhorrent that he found it necessary to refute him on almost every point. The author distinguishes "conversion of the mind" from "conversion of the heart" and concludes that preaching may affect the former to bring about a change in religion but not the latter, which would bring about a change in morals. In this author's mind, the only effective way to bring about a change in morals is good government on every level of society, one that rewards the virtuous and punishes the wicked.

---

[19] Liguori, *Letter to a Religious*, 61.

Alphonsus is concerned here only with what the author says about preaching. With respect to government, he states that this topic does not concern him and that any government, at the very least, must be subject to divine authority and not its own. He has much to say, however, when it comes to preaching. For one thing, he points out that at no place in his work does the author mention anything about grace, which alone brings about a change of heart. What is more, he points out, while there are and always will be stubborn hearts that refuse to change, that should not overshadow the many thousands upon thousands of people who have heard the Gospel preached in such a way that it has changed both their minds as well as their hearts.

Alphonsus states that the author's position is contrary to Scripture and against Church teaching: "Holy Scripture teaches us that good morals, like faith, are propagated and cultivated by preaching."[20] While he agrees with the author that bad preaching will not bring this about, he disagrees wholeheartedly when it comes to sound apostolic preaching rooted in God's Word and animated by the Spirit. Alphonsus's

---

[20] Liguori, *Refutation of a French Book*, 68.

conclusion cuts to the chase: "…the author pretends to prove that preaching has never been a useful and proper means for the reformation of morals, when, on the contrary, without preaching we should be deprived of one of the principal means destined by God to bring about the true conversion of hearts."[21]

Relevance for Redemptorist Preaching

These insights of Alphonsus on the manner and style of preaching have great relevance for today's Redemptorists and their extended family. Here are a few of those that stick out the most and come to mind most readily.

Redemptorists should always seek to preach out of humility rather than out of pride. When preaching, they must not seek to build themselves up by gaining the praise of others but allow the Holy Spirit to speak through them. They are called to be "other christs" to those they serve and should be continually asking the Lord for the grace to allow him to shine through them. They can do nothing of genuine worth without

---

[21] Liguori, *Refutation of a French Book*, 72.

God's help. He must always be in the forefront of their minds.

For Redemptorists to preach fundamental conversion of heart to others, they must first allow the good news of plentiful redemption to penetrate their own hearts, both as individuals and as a community. Their words will otherwise be hollow and ineffective. People can see through whatever masks they put on both as individuals and as a community to hide from them. Redemptorists cannot convey to others what they themselves do not possess. Whatever they say to others, they must first say to themselves and allow it to resonate in their hearts.

To be authentic preachers of God's Word, Redemptorists must foster intimate relations with the Lord through a rich life of prayer. At the heart of the Gospel message is God's desire to befriend us and enter into an intimate relationship with us. For this to happen, Redemptorists must open their hearts to him and allow his Spirit to dwell there. The best way for them to do this is to frequent the sacraments and develop a daily routine of mental prayer. Mental prayer is nothing else than meditating on the mysteries of the faith and talking to God from the heart.

Chapter Three: Preaching the Gospel

To be effective preachers, Redemptorists should prepare themselves through careful study of God's Word and the teachings of the Church. They should love learning and view it, not as an end in itself, but as a means of helping them to become effective preachers of God's Word. They should steep the writings of the Church fathers and the Church's theological tradition. At the same time, they should keep ourselves abreast of current events and seek to relate the Gospel message to the daily experiences of the people they serve.

Preaching fundamental conversion means that God's Word will have an effect not only on Redemptorist minds and hearts, but also on the way they live. Conversion, in other words, should have an effect on their moral outlook. To believe one thing in their minds and hearts and to act an entirely different way points, if nothing else, to a further need for inner conversion. When they *do* fall (and fall they will), they must fess up to their failures, rather than deny them, and seek forgiveness for their infinitely merciful Lord.

When preaching, Redemptorists should not try to display their learning with complex words and ideas that only the well-educated can understand, but speak instead in a clear, simple, and popular manner. Their goal should be to try to touch the hearts of their hearers in a way everyone can understand, regardless of their social class or level of learning. Jesus said we must become like little children to enter the kingdom of heaven (Mt 18:3). Since we are all called to be children at heart, their words, while never childish, should seek to address that deepest part of their hearts.

Finally, Redemptorists should gather at regular intervals and reflect as a community on both the content of their preaching and the manner in which we convey the Gospel message. Content and style relate to each other like matter and form. One affects the other and has an effect on the overall impact our words have on their hearers. At times, they themselves are not aware of some of the odd quirks in their preaching style. It can be very helpful if they asked others for feedback and welcomed any unsolicited comments from others, especially their confreres.

These are but a few of the many insights we can garner from Alphonsus's views on preaching. If Redemptorists are to live up to their reputation of being "kitchen priests," they must do their best not to put on any false airs and do their best to meet the faithful where they are and encourage them to take the next small step toward the conversion of their hearts and a deeper, more intimate friendship with God.

Conclusion

The charism of the Redemptorist Congregation is "to preach the Gospel to the poor and most abandoned." As members of this missionary order, Redemptorists should carefully scrutinize their approach to preaching to ensure it is an effective tool for evangelizing God's people. They should, in other words, be willing to examine both the content of what they preach and the manner in which they deliver God's message. Not to do would be negligence on their part as faithful and zealous ministers of God's Word.

The four documents examined in this chapter have given us many insights into Alphonsus's understanding of preaching and why he placed it at the heart of the Redemptorist charism. Redemptorists should take Alphonsus's views to heart and do all they can to ensure that their preaching is simple and clear, humble and unassuming, easy to understand by all who hear us, and done not to draw attention to themselves but to draw others more deeply into their relationship with Jesus, the Redeemer.

Redemptorist missionaries are called to preach Christ, not themselves. They should strive to place Christ at the center of both their personal and communal lives and be able to say with the Apostle Paul, "…it is no longer I who live, but it is Christ who lives in me" (Gal 2:20). The world today is in dire need of hearing the Gospel message of plentiful redemption in Christ. Redemptorists responded to Jesus' call to take up their cross daily and follow him (Lk 9:23). Like Alphonsus, "The Most Zealous Doctor," may they persevere in their following of Christ and commit themselves to making sure that their preaching the Gospel message of plentiful redemption is a zealous (and not half-hearted) pursuit.

Chapter Four

Plentiful Redemption

The Redemptorist motto, *Copiosa Apud Eum Redemptio*, ("With Him is Plentiful Redemption") comes from Psalm 130 verse 7 and represents the heart of the Congregation's identity and raison d'être. Having examined Alphonsus's understanding of the role of preaching in spreading the Gospel message, we can now look at the content of what is preached, and the meaning "plentiful redemption" has for Redemptorist missionary work. We shall do so by first looking at the meaning of "redemption" in Scripture and the Church's theological tradition, then seeing how the word "plentiful" extends the scope of God's redeeming grace and finally seeing its ramifications for today's Redemptorists and their extended family.

Redemption in Scripture

Old Testament. In the Old Testament, the root meaning of "redemption" has to do with payment to liberate someone in captivity. This notion extended first to family members, then to members of a person's clan or tribe, and eventually to God himself, who freed the Israelites from slavery. The central liberating event on the Old Testament was the Exodus experience, when God freed the Israelites from their bondage in Egypt and led them to the promised land across the Red Sea to live in freedom and prosper as a nation. This process of liberation involved a period of wandering in the Sinai desert where, at various points in their journey, the people turned against God, worshipped false idols, only later to repent and promise to follow the Lord God by following his commands as set forth in the Covenant given to them through Moses atop Mount Sinai. This Mosaic Covenant represents the birth of Israel as a people and provides the basis for their relationship with God.[1]

Historically, the concept of "covenant" was a political agreement between an overlord and a vassal, whereby the former promised military protection in return for the loyalty and allegiance of the latter. What is unique in the case of the Israelites is that the political tie between a vassal and his overlord was

---

[1] See Scott Hahn, gen. ed. *Catholic Bible Dictionary* (New York: Doubleday, 2009), s. v. "Redemption."

adopted and extended to the sphere of the sacred to describe the relationship between the Lord God and the Israelites as his chosen people. As far as we know, this transposition of "covenant" from the secular to the sacred was the first ever to occur in the ancient world. Although the Old Testament has other "covenants" (e.g., those with Noah, Abraham, David, and Jeremiah), the Covenant of Sinai was central to the identity of the nation of Israel and remained so during the time of Jesus and beyond.[2]

Coupled with the Hebrew notion of "Covenant" was the "Day of Atonement" (*Yom Kippur*), which, historically, during their wandering in the desert, saw the Jews selecting two goats from the flock and sacrificing one to God and sending the other into the wilderness bearing the sins of the people. A yearly occurrence, this feast recalled this time of wandering and represented the people's renewal of the Covenant. It took on special significance once the people of Israel were conquered in the sixth century, B.C., and exiled in Babylon. The promise of a New Cove-

---

[2] See Pontifical Biblical Commission, *The Bible and Morality: Biblical Roots Christian Conduct* (Vatican City: Libreria Editrice Vaticana, 2008), 26-61.

nant in the prophet Jeremiah (Jer 31:31-34) and the figure of the "Suffering Servant" in Isaiah 52-54 kept alive hope among the Jewish people that a Messiah would come at some point to liberate them from their foes and lead them once again out of slavery to freedom. *Yom Kippur* was considered one of the holiest feasts in the Jewish calendar. As the Jewish tradition developed, it became a solemn day of fasting, focusing on repentance, prayer, and forgiveness.[3]

New Testament. In Jesus' day, when the Jewish people lived under the oppression of Roman rule, the hope of a political messiah was alive and strong, especially among the Zealots who believed the time was ripe for his coming. Some, even among Jesus' own followers, thought that he was the Messiah who would liberate them from Roman oppression. These hopes would be ill-founded since Jesus saw his purpose as something far deeper. His was a message of a New Covenant, one that would free all who believed in him from the slavery of sin and lead them into the freedom of the adopted sons and daughters of his Father. He viewed himself as the Lamb of God, who

---

[3] See Hahn, *Catholic Bible Dictionary*, s. v. "Redemption."

Chapter Four: Plentiful Redemption

would take away the sins of the world by means of his passion, death, and resurrection. He also saw himself as the Suffering Servant who by his death on the cross took upon himself the sins of the people so that through his suffering and death, their own sins might be forgiven and, by his overcoming death, they themselves would one day pass through death and share in his risen and glorified humanity.[4]

The early Church would look upon the Jewish Exodus experience in an entirely different light. Conscious the various levels of meaning within God's Word, they saw it as a foreshadowing of Jesus' paschal mystery. Through the waters of Baptism, Christians were immersed in Jesus' paschal mystery and passed over from death to life. The Jewish Passover pointed to the New Passover celebrated by Jesus at the Last Supper when he offered bread and wine to his disciples as his Body and Blood. Moses, who represented the Old Law, was not allowed to enter the Promised Land. That task was given to Joshua (basically same name as Jesus' Aramaic name, "Yeshua"), who repre-

---

[4] See Pontifical Biblical Commission, *The Bible and Morality*, 62-110.

sented the New Law and the New Covenant promised to Jeremiah so many centuries before. [5]

Moreover, just as Joshua was selected by God to lead his people into the Promised Land, so too was Jesus selected by his Father in heaven to lead us beyond the pale of death into the celestial realm above. Jesus was the Lamb of God who gave up his life for the sins of the world and promised his disciples that those who ate his body and drank his blood would live forever. The Eucharist was Jesus' own Body and Blood, the Paschal Lamb and the bread from heaven that would nourish his followers spiritually and prepare them for the coming of the kingdom. Through this sacrament, this kingdom was already breaking in. The Eucharist was the sacrament of the New Creation, one that gave believers a share in Jesus' divinized humanity.[6] "God became man," as St. Athanasius of Alexandria tells us, "so that man might be-

---

[5] See John Mark Hicks, "A Christian-Theological Reading of Exodus, *Leaven* (4/1/2013), accessed August 30, 2025, https://digitalcommons.pepperdine.edu/cgi/viewcontent.cgi?article=2219&context=leaven.

[6] See John Mark Hicks, "A Christian-Theological Reading of Exodus.

come divine."[7] Whether we choose to accept this saving grace of the sacrament depends on our willingness to open our hearts and allow it to take root and penetrate the very core of our being.

Redemption in the Catholic Tradition

If Christians recognize Christ as their Redeemer, the question arises: How exactly did this Redemption take place? In the theological tradition of the Church, theologians have over the years developed three main theories to explain the meaning of what happened to Jesus of Nazareth on the cross more than two thousand years ago: (1) ransom, (2) satisfaction, and (3) instruction or moral example.

The ransom theory developed within the patristic tradition and was prevalent for the first thousand years of the Church's history. Evident in such thinkers as Augustine and Gregory the Great, it focuses on Jesus' statement in Mt 20:28 that he came "to give his life as a ransom for many." Jesus' death is understood as the ransom that God pays to Satan in order to release humanity from the chains of sin and death. This

---

[7] Athanasius of Alexandria, *On the Incarnation*, 54.3.

approach employs mythic language and sees redemption as taking place on a cosmic plane in some grand battle between the forces of Christ and those of Satan. We are nothing but passive onlookers.

The satisfaction theory, by way of contrast, was developed by Anselm of Canterbury (d. 1109) in the late eleventh-century work entitled the *Cur Deus homo*. It rejects the model of divine ransom and focuses instead on the infinite magnitude of the sin of Adam. This theory takes Satan completely out of the picture. Jesus, the expression of God's infinite compassion, dies on the cross, not to ransom us from Satan, but to satisfy the infinite demands of God's justice. Employing legal language, this theory eventually becomes the mainstay of Church teaching and remains so right up to the present. It puts humanity and God face to face. Jesus' death on the cross is understood as the way in which God's mercy satisfies the demands of God's justice. The wrath of God is quieted by his incarnate mercy.

The instruction (or moral) theory rejected both the ransom and satisfaction models as ridiculous. First developed by the scholastic theologian Peter Abelard and adopted centuries later by a number of

Chapter Four: Plentiful Redemption

the proponents of Protestant Liberalism, it insists that Jesus died on the cross not to ransom us from Satan or to satisfy God's justice, but to give us an example, i.e., to show us how to love. It uses a variety of poetic images to convey the idea that Jesus' death on the cross reveals to those who experience it the true meaning of love. Jesus' humble act of total self-surrendering love is meant to move us and evoke from us a similar response.

Although we cannot simply ignore or (worse yet) discard them, to discover the significance of the mystery of Redemption in our lives, we need to look beyond these theories our minds have concocted over the centuries. There are elements of truth in each of them and, when taken together, they give us a glimpse into the mysterious intentions of God's plan. By viewing redemption in terms of a mythic struggle between God and Satan, the ransom model focuses on the cosmic reality of *divine-human unrelation*. By putting God and humanity face to face, the satisfaction model calls attention to the element of *divine-human relation*. By bringing to the fore our own internal response to the cross, the instruction (or moral) model emphasizes the redemptive aspect of *human inner relation.* More recently, by pondering the societal implications of God's redemptive justice, liberation theologians have highlighted the element of *human social relation.* I am saying that we must not ignore these theories but try to look beyond them. Of the mystery of Christ and his cross, we must begin to ask questions that come not from the head (we are usually very good at that), but from the heart. Once we start doing that, we will find that the focus on Christ and his cross will shift from a concentration on sin and satisfaction and be understood more and more in light of God's response to human suffering.

Christ may have died to ransom us from the power of Satan, or to satisfy God's justice for Adam's sin, to teach us the ways of virtue, or perhaps even to liberate us from oppressive social structures. He may have come for some mysterious combination of all these things, which we cannot fully understand, and which is entirely known to the mind of God alone. Perhaps he came simply to be with us—to be beside us as we struggle, to suffer as we suffer, to carry the cross from which we ourselves will one day hang.

Chapter Four: Plentiful Redemption

Jesus has gone before us. He has gone through it all and is right now beside us.[8]

Of these three models of redemption, ransom held sway in the early Church and was eventually supplanted by the satisfaction model of St. Anselm, used in conjunction with Abelard's moral example model. St. Thomas Aquinas affirms Anselm's position, stating that nothing was owed to Satan to free us from the bondage of sin, but only a justice due to God alone.[9] Coupled with this insight was another: of all the ways God could have chosen for restitution, he fittingly chose to become one of us to manifest his infinite love for us. Aquinas thus uses the moral example model to complement the dominant satisfaction model and emphasize the extent of God's love and

---

[8] An expanded version of the above analysis appears in Dennis J. Billy, *Even Today: Theology and the Inner Child* (Staten Island, NY: Alba House, 1995), 73-84; See also Gustaf Aulén, *Christus Victor: An Historical Study of the Three Main Types of the Ideal of the Atonement*, trans. A. G. Herbert (New York: Macmillan, 19690, 143-59.

[9] See Thomas Aquinas, *Summa theologiae*, III, q. 48, a. 4, Ad 2m.

mercy for us.[10] Although Alphonsus uses ransom language in his writings, he does so not in the sense of a "payment to Satan," but in a sense more in line with the satisfaction model (i.e., to satisfy God's justice). He also uses it in reference to Mary as "Our Lady of Ransom," through whose intercessory prayers for us to her Son, souls are snatched from Satan's snares. What is more, while he recognizes the primary purpose of satisfying God's justice, his emphasis on plentiful redemption leads him to highlight God's willingness to suffer and die for us "in order that we may understand the great love he has for us." To verify this claim, we need only to turn to his work *Reflections and Affections on the Passion of Jesus Christ* (1751),[11] where he refers to a need to satisfy God's justice in chapter one and his infinite, bountiful love for us in

---

[10] See Thomas Aquinas, *Summa theologiae*, III, q. 1, a. 2, resp.

[11] Alphonsus de Liguori, *Reflections and Affections on the Passion of Jesus Christ* in *The Complete Works of Saint Alphonsus Liguori,* ed. Eugene Grimm vol. 5 (Brooklyn, NY. Redemptorist Fathers, 1927), 23-40.

chapter two. At one point, he even describes God as being "crazy with love" (*pazzo d'amore*) for us.[12]

Alphonsus's Understanding of "Plentiful"

Now that we have examined the meaning of redemption in both Scripture and Church tradition, we can now turn to Alphonsus's understanding of the term "plentiful." To do so, we must first understand the great influence that nominalism had on the eighteenth century Catholic theological and spiritual outlook. Made famous by William of Ockham, a fourteenth-century Franciscan scholastic theologian, nominalism denied the existence of universals and claimed that only particulars existed. This affirmation effectively deconstructed Augustine's Neoplatonic and Aquinas's Aristotelian syntheses of Catholic theology and affirmed that God himself was radically free, not bound by any moral code, and could change the content of that code at will. As a result, God's will alone determined what was Good, and it is manifested through the revelation of his Law. What

---

[12] Alphonsus de Liguori, *Reflections and Affections on the Passion of Jesus Christ*, 39-40.

followed was an emphasis in Catholic moral and spiritual theology on fulfilling God's commands.[13]

In Alphonsus's day, this approach manifested in two heterodox extremes. Jansenism, on the one hand, emphasized a strict adherence to God's law and limited access to God's grace and entry into heaven. Laxism, on the other hand, interpreted the Law freely and allowed the following of a less restrictive opinion in following God's Law. Although both views were condemned by the Church the century before, they still had great influence on the faithful of Alphonsus's day. Moreover, within Catholic orthodoxy itself, there was a conservative approach called "probabiliorism," which stated that in case of a doubt about the law the "more probable" opinion must be followed, and "probabilism," which stated that in case of a doubt one was free to follow any sound theological opinion, even if there existed other more weighty and more probable ones. Alphonsus, in turn, developed a system of "equiprobabilism," which stated that everything depended on the nature of the doubt. If it had

---

[13] See Servais Pinckaers, *The Sources of Christan Ethics*, trans. Mary Thomas Noble (Edinburg: T & Clark, 1995), 241-53.

to do with the existence of the law, then the law had not been properly promulgated, and freedom reigned. If, on the other hand, it had to do with the application of the law, then the law was in force and must be followed. It bears noting that Alphonsus's motivation in developing this approach to interpreting the Law stemmed from his desire to interpret it in a way that would allow us to be as free as possible while still being faithful to the Law.[14]

Alphonsus understood that being faithful to God's law was an essential component of living the Christian life. He also realized, however, that there was so much more to being a Christian. We should follow God's law not out of fear of being punished (servile fear), but out of love for God and his great love for us (filial fear). God's love for us, in other words, was infinite and unbounding. It was so deep that it drove him, out of his crazy love for us, to enter our world and become one of us, give himself to us completely by dying for us, and become both food and nourishment for us and a source of hope. Holiness, he believed, was not simply a matter of keeping

---

[14] See Théodule Rey-Mermet, *Alphonsus Liguori: Tireless Worker for the Most Abandoned*, 465-83.

God's commands. It also meant opening our hearts to him and being willing to enter into a deep, intimate friendship with him, one that would allow him to dwell within our heart and we in his. "Paradise for God," he once wrote, "is the heart of man."[15] With God living in our hearts, his redemptive love, Alphonsus believed, would pour out into the other dimensions of our human makeup: the physical, intellectual/psychological, spiritual, and social. Plentiful redemption, for Alphonsus, meant that the whole person would be affected by God's saving and transforming grace. Every aspect of our being would be released from the bondage of sin and made to live as free and faithful sons and daughters of God.

Implications for Redemptorists

From the above analysis, a number of characteristics of "plentiful redemption" should be dear to the hearts of all Redemptorists and their extended family.

---

[15] Alphonsus de Liguori, *The Ways to Converse Always and Familiarly with God*, 1 in *The Complete Works f Sait Alphonsus Liguori*, ed. Eugene Grimm vol. 2 (Brooklyn, NY. Redemptorist Fathers, 1926), 395.

What follows are just some of the many insights we can gain from about how we should view what this concept means for the people we serve in today's world.

If we speak of "ransom," Redemptorists should do so not in the sense of a payment to Satan, but in a derivative, metaphorical sense of God freeing us from the bondage of sin. Furthermore, although we should not underestimate the importance of Christ's redemptive death on the cross and as a way of satisfying God's justice, Redemptorists would do well to highlight it as a result of God's "crazy love" for us and his willingness to go to extravagant extents to manifest it to us.

What is more, Redemptorists should view Christ's redemption as something that extends to every dimension of our human makeup: the physical, intellectual/psychological, spiritual, and communal. With regard to the physical, they should be willing to reach out to those who are sick and poor of health, poor and marginalized, in prison, strangers, far from home, near death, and anyone who does not have the bare basics for living a dignified human life.

Regarding the intellectual/psychological dimension of our human makeup, Redemptorists should recognize that, because of the fall, our minds are darkened, our wills weakened, and our emotions out of sync and in rebellion against the gentle rule of reason's reign. At the same time, they must be conscious of the fact that Christ came to heal these wounds and transform them. For this reason, their preaching should seek to touch not only the mind, but also the heart. They should preach in such a way that we educate those we serve in the moral and spiritual truths of Christ's Gospel message and touch their hearts in such a way that they will be open to receiving him into our hearts and allowing his Spirit to dwell there.

What is more, since prayer is the great means of salvation, Redemptorists should help shape the spiritual lives of those they serve by introducing them to the various ways of prayers. Since mental prayer is morally necessary for salvation, they should encourage people to talk to God not only with their minds and hearts, but also by immersing ourselves in the silence that constantly surrounds them and in such a way that they can allow their spirits to commune with God's and, as result, enjoy the peace that comes from two close, intimate friends saying nothing and simply being with each other.

Finally, because of the communal dimension of our lives, Redemptorists should try to inculcate in the hearts of the people they serve a deep love for the Church's sacraments, especially the Eucharist. The Church's liturgy is not a private devotion, but the worship of God's people. They should encourage the faithful to look upon all other communal gatherings (e.g., prayer meetings, adoration, common rosary, novenas, etc.) as fundamentally oriented to Church's sacramental prayer and the recitation of the Divine Office. It also asks them to be concerned for the social needs of the people they serve and to make sure that they do all they can to ensure they are met. There is an intimate connection between the Church's communal worship and the call to serve the needs of our fellow human beings. To overlook one or the other represents a grave misinterpretation of the Gospel.

These are just a few of the many insights into what the phrase "plentiful redemption" should mean for today's Redemptorists and their extended family. Above all, to preach and teach plentiful redemption in today's world, Redemptorists must take care that Christ's Gospel message has taken root in their own hearts and manifested in the way they live. They must preach not only with their words, but also by their actions. Otherwise, anything they say or do will be in vain.

Conclusion

In this chapter, we have examined the meaning of "plentiful redemption" from the perspective of the meaning of "redemption" in Sacred Scripture and in the Church's theological tradition. We have found that, while he uses "ransom" language at times, Alphonsus does so in a metaphorical sense rather than in its original meaning as a payment to Satan. We have also found that, while he recognizes the primary importance of the doctrine of redemption as a means of satisfying God's justice, he prefers to present Christ's suffering and death on the cross as a way of expressing God's infinite, "crazy" love for humanity. When seen in this light, Alphonsus's understanding of the "redemption" is deeply rooted in Church teaching yet presented in a way that would touch the hearts of his hearers.

There is thus a very pastoral dimension to Alphonsus's use of redemptive language. He presents his hearers with a God who, despite their myriad flaws and failings, is madly in love with them and refuses to leave them to their own devices. He presents to them a God who has entered their world and suffered and died for them, not only to satisfy God's justice, but also to manifest his infinite love for them. The God he preaches is a "crazy God," someone who loves them more than they could ever imagine. To be sure, Jesus himself once remarked, "No one has greater love than this, to lay down one's life for one's friends" (Jn 15:13). Alphonsus's sole goal in his preaching was to convey the depths of God's love for his people and help them to respond in kind.

With all of the division, strife, and unrest present in nearly every level of human society, both within and without the Church, today's world is in dire need of hearing this message of plentiful redemption. Redemptorists and their extended family exist for no other reason than to proclaim this message, especially to the poor and most abandoned. That message must address every dimension of our human makeup: the physical, intellectual/psychological, spiritual, and communal. To preach plentiful redemption means that God wishes to heal every aspect of our human existence and transform us in such a way that we will be able to share in his divine nature through Christ's glorified humanity. As we have already seen, "God became man so that man might become divine." Let Redemptorists take Christ's promise of plentiful redemption to heart and follow in his footsteps with firm resolve.

Chapter Five

Poor and Most Abandoned

Alphonsus founded the Redemptorists to preach the Gospel message of plentiful redemption to the *poor and most abandoned*. In this final chapter of our study of Alphonsus's "Spirituality of Mission," we shall first examine his understanding of this phrase and then how Redemptorists and their extended family should apply it in today's world. For the latter, we shall examine each word in the phrase through the lens of the dimensions of our human makeup, see how they relate to each other, and apply our findings to our present situation. The aim here is to paint in broad strokes a helpful and decisive picture of where today's Redemptorists and their extended family should focus their efforts of evangelization.

The Poor and Most Abandoned in Alphonsus

We have already seen that Alphonsus had a deep daily prayer life at home and regularly attended spiritual retreats as a youth to strengthen his commitment to both God and neighbor. We have also seen that, even as a layman, Alphonsus had a deep love for the poor as evidenced in his care for the sick at the Hospital of the Incurables in Naples. This hospital was a place where those with deadly diseases and with nowhere else to go could live out their final days in relative peace and comfort. For Alphonsus, these patients were not only poor, but also abandoned by society. His personal choice to visit them reveals his desire to reach out to the poor and marginalized of Neapolitan society.

Even after he left his law practice to become a diocesan priest and a member of the Society of the Missions, Alphonsus's love for the poor of Naples (*lazzaroni*) continued to manifest itself in the "Evening Chapels" (*Capelle Serotine*). These indoor and open-air missions sought to bring the Good News to the people in the very streets where they lived. Alphonsus wanted to bring Christ to those living in the impoverished neighborhoods of the city. These encounters were filled with preaching, catechesis, hymns of praise, and sacramental healing. The aim behind them was to enliven the faith of those who, for whatever reason, had become estranged from the Church

Chapter Five: Poor and Most Abandoned

and the healing grace of Christ's salvific work present in the sacraments. These efforts at evangelization met with great success, and we could easily have seen Alphonsus continuing his ministry in this way. Such, however, would not be the case.

After some years as a diocesan priest and member of the priestly confraternity, the Apostolic Missions, and worn out by his intense schedule of mission preaching in the city of Naples, Alphonsus went south to the town of Scala on the Amalfi coast to make retreat and recuperate from his heavy workload. He stayed at the Casa Anastasio, a small chapel and villa on the hilly outskirts of Scala, where he encountered poor and illiterate peasant shepherds, who knew little of the faith and had scarce, if any, access to the sacraments. Deeply touched by their need for pastoral care, Alphonsus made it his mission to reach out to these abandoned souls by gathering a band of followers who would dedicate their lives to bringing the Good News to the abandoned poor on remote hilltop villages of the kingdom. He envisioned a traveling mission band that would stay for an extended period of time to renew the faith through preaching, catechesis, and administering the sacraments. They would leave behind practices such as meditation and prayer before the Blessed Sacrament to keep the faith alive until their return sometime later to continue the renewal of the people's faith. In this way, the Gospel would be preached by Word and Sacrament to those who needed to hear it most.

We must remember that, at the time, the Kingdom of Naples did not suffer from any shortage of priests. Although historical records do not give a precise number, the city was known to have an abundance of priests.[1] The problem was that very few wished to leave the comforts of a cosmopolitan life to minister in the kingdom's distant hinterland. Alphonsus's desire to minister to the poor and most abandoned in the city of Naples now shifted to these neglected countryside villages. He saw a need that was not being met and decided to fill it. He saw that some people were more abandoned than others and felt moved to minister in those places where no one else wanted to go. When seen in this light, Alphonsus understood the phrase "poor and most abandoned" as

---

[1] For the Neapolitan clergy of Alphonsus's day, see Rey-Mermet, *St. Alphonsus: Tireless Worker for the Most Abandoned*, 37, 130-31.

meaning "both/and" rather than "either/or." He saw that there were poor and abandoned in both the city and in the remote countryside but chose to minister to the latter because of the outstanding need. He experienced firsthand that some needs were more pronounced than others. He saw that there were poor and abandoned almost everywhere but wanted to serve those who were *most* abandoned.

Today's Poor and Most Abandoned

We should acknowledge at the outset that Alphonsus's understanding of "the poor and most abandoned" was influenced by his historical and cultural surroundings and that the Redemptorist interpretation of it today will be affected by similar factors. Alphonsus's activity, for example, was limited to the kingdom of Naples and, if it had not been for St. Clement Hofbauer and others, who brought this fledgling congregation across the Alps to Poland, then Austria and, from there, throughout the rest of Europe and beyond, the Redemptorists might never have developed the way they did in later years. What is more, Alphonsus lived at a time when there was not a shortage of priests but only of missionary zeal. This situation is very different from today's experience where, in many parts of the Catholic world, priestly vocations are few and far between. Similarly, the political situation in the more than 100 countries where they serve can range anywhere from democratic republics to constitutional monarchies to Communist dictatorships and to places where the Catholic population is a small, persecuted minority. With such a variety of historical and cultural circumstances, perhaps the best approach for understanding the meaning of the phrase today would be to examine each part of the phrase—*poor* and *most abandoned*—through the lens of the various dimensions of our human makeup: the physical, intellectual/psychological, spiritual, and communal. Let us see what this interpretative approach has to offer.

The Poor. It is possible to be rich in some areas of our personal makeup, yet poor in others. There are, for example, the materially poor who live beneath the accepted standard of living in any given society. Even here, we must recognize that this standard of living varies from country to country. What is considered "poor" in the Unted States or Europe, for example, will likely differ from what it means in the developing world. What is more, even within developed, industrialized countries, there are many nuances that need to be considered. There is a difference, moreover, between a family that for generations has been caught in a downward spiral of economic hardship due to race, education, and unjust social structures, and those who from rich and middle-class backgrounds have fallen into homelessness due to mental illness, addiction to drugs, or family dysfunction. For this reason, Redemptorists and their extended family need to be aware of the various factors that cause, promote, and perpetuate material poverty. Not to do so would be to minimize the factors behind such impoverishment and thus fail to address the root causes behind it.

Similarly, a person may not be materially poor but suffer from intellectual or psychological impoverishment. In addition to those who are mentally disabled from birth, some may come from working families able to provide shelter and put food on the table but do not emphasize the need to cultivate the mind through education and reading. Such people may have highly refined skills badly needed by society but little knowledge of the faith. When coupled with poor emotional and social skills, they are often unable to enter into meaningful relationships with others. They may lead highly productive lives on one level of their human makeup but are deeply lacking in one of the most important dimensions of what it means to be human: the intellectual and psychological. For this reason, they never develop their full potential as human beings since they have neglected to foster in their lives a healthy inner world that puts their unruly emotions in sync with the gentle rule of reason's reign. They may be highly successful in business but out of touch with their emotions and inept in their ability to form close, intimate relationships. They hunger for something that the material world cannot supply and, if not helped out of their inner poverty, are doomed to live lonely, unfulfilled lives.

What is more, a person can be both materially well off and have a rich inner life but have lost touch with the sacred. Such a person has little or no sense of anything lying beyond the physical world. The notion of God is a figment of the human imagination and has no place in his or her mind whatsoever. All that exists is what one can verify empirically. To speak of something beyond this world is, at best, wishful thinking and, at worse, self-deceptive and delusionary. Such a person may say he or she has a spiritual life because of a rich inner world, yet it is open not to a transcendent, personal God but, at best, to a projection of oneself onto the realm of the sacred. Such spiritual poverty is a far cry from those whom Jesus blesses as the "poor in spirit," that is, people who believe in God, have a personal relationship with him, and recognize in all humility that everything they have comes from him. Those who do not believe in any kind of transcendent reality, let alone a personal God who created, redeemed, and sanctifies them out of his infinite love for them, should be the object of prayers that ask God to bring about in their lives a genuine conversion of heart. Only the grace of God can penetrate the various defenses they have put in place to ward off his loving advances.

A person can be rich in every other dimension of his or her human makeup, except that of the communal. This can mean a variety of things. First, it could point to an inability to form sound human relationships on nearly every level of human interaction (e.g., family, school, parish, local community, etc.) because of a lack of emotional maturity. Such an instance points to the interrelated nature of all the anthropological dimensions of our existence. It could also mean that the person is trapped by unjust social structures that hinder or even prevent sound human advancement and upward social mobility. Such structures point to the analogous nature of sin which is, at one and the same time universal (i.e., original sin), personal (i.e., actual mortal or venial sin), and social (i.e., societal sin).[2] Since we are social beings by nature we all participate in this latter dimension in some way shape or form. For this reason, today's Redemptorists and their extended family need to be conscious of the ways in which they and others participate (perhaps even unknowingly) in these unjust societal structures and work to liberate or at least alleviate those who have lived under and been oppressed by them.

Redemptorists must be sensitive to the poverty in their midst on whatever level it exists and, like our zealous founder, be willing to confront it wherever and whenever they find it. Most of all, they must be

---

[2] See *Compendium of the Social Doctrine of the Church*, nos. 115-23.

Chapter Five: Poor and Most Abandoned 99

sensitive to the fact that these dimensions of our human makeup—the physical, intellectual/psychological, spiritual, and communal—are all interrelated and can exist in different degrees and in various combinations in the various groups of people they are called to serve. They must prudently seek to discern the different kinds of poverty that exist in any particular place and time, and they must be willing to reach out to those in need and seek to alleviate them and provide for their needs.

Most Abandoned. The phrase, "most abandoned," consists of two elements and seems to imply that some people are more abandoned than others. We see this distinction operative in Alphonsus's own decisions in pastoral ministry since we find him moving at various moments in his life from ministering to the patients in the Hospital of the Incurables to the *lazzaroni* in the slums of Naples to the poor sheepherders of the remote hilltop villages in the southern Italian countryside. It seems that what qualified as *most* abandoned, for him, were those who were not only materially poor, but also without someone to preach the Good News and administer the sacraments to them, thus giving them little or no access to Christ's healing and transforming grace. As we have seen in the previous section, poverty applies not only to a person's material assets but also to one or more of any of the other dimensions of their human makeup. The questions we must now ask ourselves are: How can we identify those who are poor today in one or more of these dimensions? Has the Church neglected them in any way? And, if so, how can the Redemptorists and their extended family minister to their needs?

We live in a vastly different period of history from Alphonsus's. He lived before the industrial revolution, the digital age, and the onslaught of artificial intelligence. These technological innovations have had a great impact on the way we view ourselves and how we relate to others. People today can easily bury themselves in their cellphones or surfing the internet or spending endless hours on video games, or on a host of other digital activities without interacting with anyone. As a result, they can have poor social skills and feel lonely and isolated. With the rise of robotics, the time will come (and, for some, already has) when people will try to replace genuine human relationships with artificial ones. In many respects, the brave new world of Aldous Huxley has already arrived and, for others, is just on the horizon.

The effects of these technological innovations on the human person are many and varied. Those who spend an inordinate amount of time burying themselves in video games, for example, can gain an unhealthy amount of weight due to poor eating habits and lack of exercise. Surfing the internet for mindless (often risky) entertainment can numb a person's intellectual prowess and make him or her a slave to the computer or cell phone and doomed to live in bondage to whatever unverified (possibly false) information they encounter. Allowing a cellphone to become an extension of ourselves can keep us from interacting with others in more personal, intimate ways. If Redemptorists are not careful, they themselves can lose their sense of the sacred by existing in the world of cyberspace and eventually losing touch with the world around them. God's creation gradually cedes into the background of their awareness as they lose themselves a digital world of their own or (worse yet) of someone else's making. If they are not watchful and discerning, they can easily allow this digital world to reign over their every whim, as it becomes their master and they its undutiful servants.

The Church needs to respond to the challenges of the present by discerning the most prudent and effective ways to minister to the needs of the people today. It must look at the challenges of the virtual world not by running away from it but by entering into it in meaningful ways and seeking to transform it from the inside-out. "Grace perfects nature," as the saying goes, and the Church needs to enter the world of cyberspace so that the Gospel can be preached in a way that touches the hearts of those within it and call them to an intimate friendship with Jesus. It needs to find new ways of proclaiming the Gospel message in the virtual world. Jesus entered our world some two thousand years ago in order to heal it of its sinful wounds, transform it, and make of it a new creation. In a similar way, he desires to enter this virtual world of ours and transform it into a place where sin has no place and where his Spirit can abide. Just as Jesus raised Lazarus from the dead and called him out of the darkness of the tomb (Jn 11:38-44), so too must his Church speak words of life to those who have been hypnotized by the allures of this virtual reality and call them back to their senses so that they can continue living in the real world in order to help in its ongoing transformation. This virtual world, in other words, needs to be baptized and brought to life in Christ so that the forces of evil will not overtake it with its unethical and unlawful filth (e.g., the dark web, pornography, sex trafficking, cyberbullying, identity theft, etc.). The kingdom of Light must enter this virtual world, exorcise it of its demons, and make it a safe place to travel and explore.

Conclusion: Going Forth

Redemptorists and their extended family must remain faithful to their charism of preaching the Good News of plentiful redemption to the poor and most abandoned. They must do so, however, conscious of the historical and cultural situations in which they find themselves and aware of the challenges facing today's Church. That means having recourse not only to the traditional methods of mission preaching, retreat work, writing, spiritual direction, missionary outreach, and parish ministry (to name but a few), but also being willing to experiment with new methods of evangelization that can reach the neglected and hard to access areas in today's world.

Unlike Alphonsus, many Redemptorists live in areas that are both badly in need of priests and have difficulty meeting even the ordinary needs of the people in the local parishes. The physical, intellectual/psychological, spiritual, and communal needs of the people, moreover, will vary from place to place according to the economic, cultural, political, societal, and linguistic contexts in which they serve. Like Jesus, Redemptorists must be willing to enter the world of those around them, give of themselves completely, and to become nourishment and a source of hope for them. Alphonsus strove to do so in his own day and age; Redemptorists and their extended family must seek the same in theirs. They do so by responding creatively to the challenges of their day and seeking to evangelize not only the real world in which they find themselves, but also the digital, virtual world that has so deeply influenced both themselves and the minds and hearts of the people they serve. How can this be done? The Beauty of the Gospel may be of some help, and Alphonsus himself may give us a clue.

The founder of the Redemptorists was not only a great preacher, moral theologian, and spiritual writer, but also a talented artist, musician, and poet. His hymn *Tu Scendi dalle Stelle* ("You Descend from the Stars") remains to this day the most celebrated Christmas carol in all of Italy. His paintings of the Madonna and the Crucifixion of Christ were meant to engage the sympathy of those beholding them and bring them to prayer. His poems in honor of Jesus and his Mother Mary, many of which he also put to music, display a deep awareness of their love for humanity and the humility behind their actions.[3] Alphonsus sought to use the arts as a way of touching people's hearts and drawing them closer to the Lord. Redemptorists and their extended family should seek to do the same not only by means of the arts that were at Alphonsus's disposal in his day, but also by having recourse to film, podcasts, social media, and the like, to bring God's message to the poor and most abandoned of their day. In doing so, they will be able to reach those who perhaps have never set foot in a church, attended Mass, read the Scriptures, or had

---

[3] See, for example, Rey-Mermet, *St. Alphonsus: Tireless Worker for the Most Abandoned*, 75-87.

the Good News shared with them. Jesus himself once said, "The harvest is plentiful, but the laborers are few" (Mt 9:37). There are many areas (both real and virtual) in today's world where the Lord is calling for laborers to the harvest. May the Redemptorists and their extended family respond to this call by walking in Jesus' footsteps under the inspiration of Alphonsus, their founder.

Conclusion

As we conclude our treatment of the "Spirituality of Mission," let us remember that it represents only a single aspect of St. Alphonsus's understanding of Redemptorist spirituality. As we have seen earlier in this book and in previous presentations, we can liken his spirituality to a two-edged sword, in which one edge represents a "Spirituality of Practice," the other, a "Spirituality of Heart," both of which come together in the single point of a "Spirituality of Mission." When seen in this light, mission presupposes a stable and committed pattern of holy exercises that seek to penetrate the heart, bring about fundamental conversion (*metanoia*), and lead to a desire to go forth and share the Gospel message with others. Without these two edges of the sword, any missionary attempt will have little force and will, in the end, be ultimately pointless.

In this book, we have examined Alphonsus's "Spirituality of Mission" from the perspective of the single, culminating point of a double-edged sword comprised of holy exercises that move the heart to action regarding the "poor and most abandoned." We have looked at what this phrase meant for Alphonsus in his own historical context and attempted to see what it might mean for today's Redemptorists and their extended family. We have done so by looking at the phrase through the lens of the dimensions of our human makeup—the physical, intellectual/psychological, spiritual, and communal—and noticed that what we see will vary according to the historical and cultural contexts in which we serve.

Redemptorists and their extended family inhabit a very different world from Alphonsus's. He lived in a time that preceded the invention of photography, telephones, radio, cars, planes, television, moving pictures, the internet, email, cell phones, artificial intelligence, and many other modern conveniences. While these modern technologies have influenced our self-understanding in many ways, we still remain men, women, and children capable of entering into an intimate relationship with Christ. For this reason, the Gospel message of calling people to a fundamental conversion of heart (*metanoia*) remains as relevant today as it was during Alphonsus's time. The challenge for Redemptorists and their extended family today is to engage the world in constructive and creative ways that will help people to get in touch with their deep inner yearnings and enable them to see that these cannot be satisfied by anything or anyone but God himself. Jesus brought the message of his Father's unconditional love to the world some 2,000 years ago. While that message itself has never changed, the way in which it is communicated must be adapted so that those alive today can hear it, allow it to touch them, and take it to heart. May the followers of Alphonsus embrace his "Spirituality of Mission," make it their own, and do their best to bring the message of Christ's redeeming love to today's poor and most abandoned.

www.ingramcontent.com/pod-product-compliance
Lightning Source LLC
Chambersburg PA
CBHW071955070426
42453CB00008BA/796